THE CAREGIVER'S JOURNAL

My Book of Memories

©2022 Jascinth Brockington

MY NAME (THE CAREGIVER)

_____

MEMORIES OF (MY LOVED ONE)

_____

Start Date

_____

TABLE OF CONTENTS

		PAGE
FOREWORD		4
SECTION 1:	Flowers While They Live: One Day at a Time	6
SECTION 2:	I Remember You with Love	10
SECTION 3:	I Will Always Love You!	17
SECTION 4:	The Final Days	20
	The Necessary Grieving	25
	The Necessary Forgiving	29
	The Necessary Closure	33
	How I Overcame	38
SECTION 5:	Treasured Memories	39
	Special Memories Picture Collection	42
	A Reservoir of Emotions	52
SECTION 6:	Living Without You	60
	Sample Poem	66
SECTION 7:	A Time to H-E-A-L	68
CONCLUSION:		76

The Caregiver's Journal – Brockington, J. ©2022 Pg. 3

FOREWORD (Jascinth Brockington)

Always give them their flowers while they live. Flowers from the perspective of caregiving means any kind of giving—literal gifts, including flowers—but, even more so, the giving of respect and appreciation to your mother, father or loved one for whom you are caring. The caregiver carries a very heavy load—the load of giving time and attention to all the needs of a loved one, in many cases. And so, to all caregivers, I applaud you.

You would be shocked at the number of people who have the ability yet refuse to take care of their loved ones—even their own parents! I've heard so many stories of caregiving—or the lack thereof—across the board. There are those on the one end of the spectrum who take on the responsibility of giving care to both parents. I've heard stories of this scenario ending well, or not, or how many caregivers who lose their sanity in the process, so much so that they themselves require therapy or mental care; or those who barely make it through the days or the months, or years, required to care for their loved ones!

Throughout your journal, I will interject words of encouragement to you—specifically to those caregivers who chose or are now choosing to take care of their loved ones at home, as I did. I am convinced this is the most difficult of all the choices. Not just because it was our family's collective choice, and I was the one who opted to provide the at-home caregiving. But…it just is. All caregivers can and do concur: It's a heavy load.

There is no easy caregiving and none without its own sets of challenges. Therefore, you are a star, and here is your flower while you live and, at some point, have sacrificed for a loved one.

SECTION 1: Flowers While They Live—One Day at a Time

If you're wondering whether or not I have experience losing a close loved one, the answer is a definitive "YES!" I do have first-hand experience. Not just the experience of losing a close loved one, but also the excruciating experience of losing two loved ones—in my case, both my parents—in the very same year!

I was the immediate, at-home caregiver for my mother, as she was living at home with me, but my father's passing was completely unexpected. The most difficult part was that he was living in another country...and in the middle of COVID-19. By the time I or any of my siblings could even plan a trip to get there, having to wade through all the rigors of traveling during the pandemic, my father had already passed.

That experience will never leave me, and please know that with the consolation and encouragement that I convey in this journaling experience—to you—I fully understand the painstaking journey of caregiving even after that initial decision to give care.

So, the trip to Jamaica after my father's passing was made by two of my sisters, with the intention to learn the intricacies, while girding up our loins and doing what we needed to do, all simultaneously. This was brand new to us. We had not been faced with having to plan a parent's funeral before, and the time that our dad's unexpected death occurred was like a double punch to the gut to us. We had to make funeral arrangements, closing business ventures, securing properties, selling assets, and a host of other necessities, on the one hand. Then, on the other hand, we were providing care to our mother, who, by that time was receiving Hospice Care—*in my home*. Throughout the challenges, the sleepless nights, still having to work and take care of various responsibilities, one major thing I could hold onto was the feeling that I had help. Not too long ago, I prayed for a friend of mine who shared with me how she had to do it alone. She was an only child. I prayed for her because I had two siblings who were nurses and who would completely take care of the *medical* aspects and medical decisions concerning our mother. My friend had none of that. She did it all with outside help, having to pay astronomical amounts of money, while dealing with the changes and the needs of her father.

I remember telling her that all she could do was to take it one day at a time, cherish all the remaining time she had with her dad and to love on him by giving him his flowers—that is, to celebrate him—while he still lived. My experiences as a caregiver, combined with my friend's courage, provided the inspiration for this book. As you proceed to engage in documenting and preserving this reservoir of memories of your loved one, make sure to date your entries throughout the journal.

SECTION 2: I Remember You With Love!

Remembering can sometimes be a negative; but I do believe that most of the time, remembering can be a huge positive! Since all of this speaks of action—intentional action—let us do a "remembering" exercise. This, and the next section, will encourage you, the Caregiver, and give you the opportunity to positively remember your loved one.

My grandmother used to say to us: "*Count your blessings and name them one by one…and it will surprise you what the Lord has done…*"

I have taken that to heart for all my life, and even as an adult who takes notice of everything from a critical perspective—and with attention to details—I know that our circumstances can seem to be hopeless and life-destroying. Losing a loved one can be at the top of that list of negative circumstances. The death—or any kind of loss—of loved ones can hold positive memories, however. I truly believe that! Those memories can be etched into our hearts and souls forever.

With this guided exercise, please take the time to **write down positive memories** which have been etched into your heart and soul. Tell the story in your own unique way:

I remember the time(s) we smiled or laughed together

_____
_____
_____
_____
_____
_____
_____
_____
_____
_____
_____
_____
_____
_____
_____
_____
_____

The last time we hugged, I was … and you were…

I remember our last *very* serious talk…

I remember how talented you were…

You were able to:

I remember the last meal you cooked for me (us)…

I remember the last time we traveled together. Our trip was…

_____
_____
_____
_____
_____
_____
_____
_____
_____
_____
_____
_____
_____
_____
_____
_____
_____
_____
_____
_____

SECTION 3: I Will Always Love You!

Still in the mode of "Remembering" your loved one, this section will guide you, the Caregiver, into remembering how much you loved, admired, and cherished your loved one.

One of my all-time favorite songs was made popular by singer, the late Whitney Houston, called "Always Love You."

This is a two-part exercise.

For the first part, I want YOU to IMAGINE your loved one singing this verse to you:

"***Bitter-sweet memories, that is all I'm taking with me. So, goodbye, please don't cry***…I've lived life to the best of my ability…no regrets. Be strong and live the rest of your days as if only one day remains."

For the second part of this exercise, I want YOU to SING out loud, as if your loved one is there listening to you serenading him or her:

"...***And I will always love you, I will always love you...I will always love you***! Beloved, take your rest!"

Add anything you want to say personally about your love for him/her...

_____
_____
_____
_____
_____
_____
_____
_____
_____
_____
_____

SECTION 4: The Final Days

Many people have taken on the responsibility of caring for their loved ones at home—as opposed to placing him or her in a healthcare facility. I think it is a blessing if you are able to take care of your loved ones at home. While I'm very much aware that for so many people this is not an option, I do believe that, when possible, this is the very best thing for our loved ones. I speak from personal experience in relation to that choice as well. I also believe that the caregiver will receive a special blessing in doing this, if this *is at all* possible.

Such is my personal story and that of my family's in taking care of our mother.

At the beginning, my mother displayed moments of forgetfulness. And because she had one of the sharpest and most witty minds I knew—with an unmatched memory capacity—it became obvious that something was happening. In the space of a few months, she could no longer travel on her own; soon thereafter, she could not be left home by herself. When I started taking her to a sitter—who happened to be the daughter of her best friend—she would protest at first. Eventually it became a part of our daily routine for me to drop her off at the sitter's home on my way to work.

Immediately before the Covid-19 pandemic was globalized, I began taking my mother with me everywhere that I went, and since my sister and I had started a healthcare facility—an adult daycare center—I would have my mother with me all day long, every day. She literally became a child again.

My mother's final days had her in Hospice care, and she was still with me, at home. We arranged for a hospice bed to be brought in, and she was in my living room for approximately 14 months before she passed away in December of 2021.

I'm of the opinion—and irrevocably convinced—that the best place for our loved ones in their last and final days is at home with *their loved ones*. However, as I stated before, that arrangement is not possible for everyone and for a myriad of reasons.

On the next couple pages, for those whose elderly loved ones are still with you, write down the plans which you have put in place for their final days. Give consideration to the possibility of having your loved one spend his or her final days at home, if at all possible. Write down the details of what that would look like for your family.

In the event they have already passed, then just notate some details of their final days as you remember them—if only for the sake of documenting memories of your loved one:

Notes concerning your loved one's **Final Days**:

_____

_____

_____

_____

_____

_____

_____

_____

_____

_____

_____

_____

_____

_____

_____

_____

_____

The Necessary Grieving

In the case of death and dying, it is now my realization that just as there are different ways that a person could die—*die we all must.* At the time of completing this book for publication, the Bishop at my home church had passed a few months ago, on the *exact* date as my mother, one year later. It might as well have been only one day apart. That's what it felt like, having lost my father *and* my mother in one year, then a spiritual mentor a year later. It had me right at the verge of asking God "*Why*"?

The way in which we die, of course, could determine the level of trauma—for the ones left behind. Therefore, a person's grieving can sometimes be measured by the level of trauma felt at the death of his or her loved ones. Factors such as age, relation (i.e., parent, child, sibling, relative, or close friend), the cause of death, etcetera, all determine the level of trauma experienced by surviving loved ones upon that death. I believe, then, that in traumatic situations, no matter the level, there should be the space and time taken to grieve. It is a necessity. And no matter how strong you as a caregiver thinks that you are, you still need to take time to grieve. I've heard it said that sometimes caregivers grieve while the loved ones are yet alive. I truly believe that was my experience. Maybe it was because I had moments of just breaking down, when I realized that my mom's condition was worsening, and it was just a matter of time before she would be gone. As she declined more and more, it became less difficult.

My strategy became spending more time talking to her—even when she could no longer speak. I talked to her, read, and sang to her.

Over the next couple pages, make notes regarding your method of grieving. If your loved one is still alive, do some research to see what the experts recommend, and if your loved one is deceased, make note of some of the helpful strategies you used **during your time of grieving** that could possibly help someone else.

_____

_____

_____

_____

_____

_____

_____

_____

_____

_____

The Necessary Forgiving

Forgiving is seldom ever one-sided. In fact, I believe it is most effective when it is recognized as 3-fold. There is the need to forgive yourself, the need to ask for forgiveness from the other person, and the need for *you* to forgive the person. All three steps are critical. The importance of forgiveness has been dummied down in recent years. The need to feel justified and "right" has increased enormously in our culture. And there is nothing more brutal, or in greater opposition to the act of forgiveness, than a person feeling that he or she is the one in the *right*. This can become so chronic that you will never ever feel the need to seek forgiveness. But like everything else, it requires practice to accomplish this. And, like everything else, practicing 3-fold forgiveness makes it a perfect and permanent virtue. It's only the coupling of self-centeredness and pride that keeps us from having a forgiving heart.

Bar the existence of deep pride, asking someone to forgive you is far easier than forgiving yourself. A March 2022 BetterUp.com blog states, "*You likely weren't taught how to forgive yourself. As a result, you struggle to move on when you've let yourself down. Forgiving others can feel much easier than forgiving ourselves*" (BetterUp.com).

In the case of giving care to a loved one, all 3-fold forgiveness is necessary to get to that place of release—both for them and for you. In most cases of giving care to a loved one, there is the need for 3-fold forgiveness. Consider your personal situation, in relation to your loved one, and **write down your experience with forgiving or receiving forgiveness** (even from yourself).

The Necessary Closure

Closure does not mean forgetting. However, what it means, for each person's situation, is the ability, time and opportunity which will allow the grieving person to move on. For the millions of us who have experienced these losses, it could very well mean *many millions of differences* in what "closure" looks like. I have told you my story of losses, and for friends of mine, and for other family members experiencing simultaneous losses. I can also tell you with certainty that *each* has "closure" defined and construed differently.

Your experience is valuable, far more than you know. The idea of this journal is that you will document and be able to use this as therapy for yourself. But in addition to that, I believe you can help others who will one day be faced with losses—who may not know what to do while living the experience. Your documentation through the end of that journey could mean a wealth of knowledge for someone newly facing those experiences and embarking upon his or her own journey.

So, think about it for a while, then consider taking the next couple of pages to document your interpretation of what "Closure" is, and is not. Conduct your own mini-researches, even. There is a plethora of testimonies, whether on Facebook, YouTube, or other platforms—in video format, and in written formats to glean from—and get a feel for what others are doing and are going through. Many people have already gone through this and those would make for great examples of courage, strength, and the ability to overcome. Consider even more so the techniques used which served to empower the Caregiver(s) to show exemplary victory. All of this will one day be extremely valuable to someone else with whom you will share.

Our experiences are never unique, although this one is happening to *you*, happening to *your* loved one, and happening specifically to *your* family. Yet, there are people out there who have gone through it, are going through it, or are on their way to experiencing what you're going through right now, as it relates to taking care of a loved one.

Just as you will be able to help someone else after this experience, so, too, will others that you help through their journey be able to extend help to others.

Write out your thoughts concerning "Closure."

CLOSURE (What it is)

_____

_____

CLOSURE (What it is not)

My Plan to Share My "Victory" (How I Overcame)

_____
_____
_____
_____
_____
_____
_____
_____
_____
_____
_____
_____
_____
_____
_____
_____
_____
_____
_____
_____

The Caregiver's Journal – Brockington, J. ©2022 Pg. 38

SECTION 5: Treasured Memories

This is where you get the opportunity to collect as many pictures as possible, to insert into your journal. The saying goes: *"A picture is worth a thousand words"* and this has been proven true time and time again. In this era of digital photos and galleries, and almost no such thing as *physical pictures* anymore, you could possibly be one who literally has no photos at all to work with here! I understand, because, again, we're living in a digital era. I would be hard-pressed to find a young person today who even knows what a photo album is! I understand this, too, because as much as I still have photo albums, they are hidden under other books and may have been there for many years. So, if need be, and if I dig far enough, I'm sure I could still get my hands on *paper* photos.

If that is also true for you, this project is already halfway done. Size and place the photos in the frames on the next

10 upcoming pages. But, if you do not have existing photos, this is what I want you to do: *Simply select *ANY 10 photos* of your loved one(s) from your smart phone; send them off for printing. When the pictures are returned, crop them as needed, and tape them into your journal for a long-lasting gallery of physical pictures and memories of your loved one(s). There is nothing to me like taking out a photo album from many years ago and browsing through it at a random moment. It can sometimes be very sentimental, but even for those *macho* men and women, who never cry, I challenge you to create a physical gallery of your loved ones! I promise—it will change your lives forever!

Special Memories - Picture 1

Title/Caption_____

_____
_____
_____
_____
_____

Special Memories - Picture 2

Title/Caption _____

_____

_____

_____

_____

_____

_____

_____

Special Memories - Picture 3

Title/Caption_____

_____

_____

_____

_____

_____

_____

Special Memories - Picture 4

Title/Caption_____

_____
_____
_____
_____
_____

Special Memories - Picture 5

Title/Caption _____

_____
_____
_____
_____
_____
_____

Special Memories - Picture 6

Title/Caption_____

_____

_____

_____

_____

_____

Special Memories - Picture 7

Title/Caption _____

_____
_____
_____
_____
_____
_____

Special Memories - Picture 8

Title/Caption_____

_____

_____

_____

_____

_____

_____

The Caregiver's Journal – Brockington, J. ©2022 Pg. 49

Special Memories - Picture 9

Title/Caption _____

_____
_____
_____
_____
_____
_____

Special Memories - Picture 10

Title/Caption_____

_____

_____

_____

_____

_____

_____

The Caregiver's Journal – Brockington, J. ©2022 Pg. 51

A Reservoir of Emotions

Just as I was certain you could achieve the goal of printing physical photos for your journal, I am also certain that with each photo there exists a memory. If your loved one has passed, even more so, there likely exists sadness as well as joy as you view the photos. I have been in that exact place—and it has not been too many months ago, either. So, I'm fully aware of the possible level of sadness, a seeming reservoir of tears, happy and/or sad memories.

This next exercise is a simple one. **Write down** the emotions you feel as you look at each photo of your loved one. To the best of your ability, and using the previous descriptions/captions for each, make note of the emotions that you associate with the picture of your loved one. Maybe you recall the exact setting of the photo where something special occurred—happy, sad, memorable, even hilarious!

Maybe there are other elements of the picture—other persons in the shot with your loved one, for example—that trigger an emotion, or several significant emotions.

Dig deep to recall as much details as possible, to create this significant memory section.

PICTURE #1 makes me feel _____

Write the EMOTION above, then **Explain Below:**

_____

_____

_____

_____

_____

_____

_____

_____

_____

_____

_____

PICTURE #2 makes me feel _____

Write the EMOTION above, then **Explain Below:**

_____

_____

_____

_____

_____

_____

_____

_____

_____

PICTURE #3 makes me feel _____

Write the EMOTION above, then **Explain Below:**

_____

_____

_____

The Caregiver's Journal – Brockington, J. ©2022 Pg. 54

_____
_____
_____
_____
_____
_____
_____
_____
_____
_____

PICTURE #4 makes me feel _____

Write the EMOTION above, then **Explain Below:**

_____
_____
_____
_____
_____
_____
_____
_____
_____
_____
_____
_____
_____

PICTURE #5 makes me feel _____

Write the EMOTION above, then **Explain Below:**

_____
_____
_____
_____
_____
_____
_____
_____
_____
_____
_____

PICTURE #6 makes me feel _____

Write the EMOTION above, then **Explain Below:**

_____
_____
_____
_____
_____
_____
_____

PICTURE #7 makes me feel _____

Write the EMOTION above, then **Explain Below:**

PICTURE #8 makes me feel _____

Write the EMOTION above, then **Explain Below:**

_____
_____
_____
_____
_____
_____
_____
_____
_____
_____
_____
_____

PICTURE #9 makes me feel _____

Write the EMOTION above, then **Explain Below:**

_____
_____
_____
_____
_____
_____
_____
_____
_____
_____
_____
_____

PICTURE #10 makes me feel _____

Write the EMOTION above, then **Explain Below:**

_____
_____
_____
_____
_____
_____
_____
_____
_____
_____
_____
_____
_____

SECTION 6: Living Without You

Four months after my Mom passed away, my niece gave birth to a beautiful little girl. What was amazing to me about the baby girl was not just that she looked a lot like her great-grandmother (my Mom), but that she also had some of the exact facial expressions that my Mom had. It was incredulous to watch as she would frown, then immediately laugh out—just like my Mom used to do. Then she would stare you down, if you were speaking too loudly, and would not blink for what seemed like forever.

My Mom was known to do that even in trying to scold us—and she would have us cracking up laughing. If there is such a thing as twin-spirits, I would believe this to be one of those incredible cases!

If you could come up with sentences that summarize characteristics of your loved one—whether or not he or she has passed yet—make a note of it below:

_____

_____

_____

_____

_____

_____

_____

_____

_____

_____

_____

If your loved one has passed, use the next few spaces to

write sentiments of special things you miss, not having him or her around.

I Miss Our Talks About:

_____

_____

_____

_____

_____

_____

_____

_____

_____

_____

I Miss Our Trips To:

_____
_____
_____
_____
_____
_____
_____
_____
_____
_____
_____
_____

We Did These Things Together:

_____
_____
_____
_____
_____
_____
_____

The Caregiver's Journal – Brockington, J. ©2022 Pg. 63

I Miss Singing These Songs Together:

My Happiest Memories Of You Are:

_____

_____

_____

_____

_____

_____

_____

_____

_____

_____

_____

_____

_____

_____

_____

_____

SAMPLE POEM

<u>My Special **Poem** to Describe *Life Without You*</u>

©*2021 Jascinth Brockington*

The song says: *Rainy Days and Mondays*
Always Get Me Down They Make Me Cry…
When I remember you, it makes me cry, yes.
But many times it makes me smile too,
And I know now that crying has a dual value.
It can sometimes happen when I feel sad,
That's when I'm missing you, and at other times,
When I remember the many happy times with you.
Rainy days still make me cry, and maybe Mondays, too,
But Mom, you gave us life, and you lived a beautiful life because you shared yourself with so many people!
As God had blessed you with us, so too did He blessed us with you.
And I will always love you.

- Your Daughter, *Jascinth*

WRITE A POEM TO YOUR LOVED ONE

A Special **Poem** to Describe *Life Without You*

_____
_____
_____
_____
_____
_____
_____
_____
_____
_____
_____
_____
_____
_____
_____

Your _____, _____

The Caregiver's Journal – Brockington, J. ©2022 Pg. 67

SECTION 7: A Time to H-E-A-L

There is a statement in the Bible which says: *"A cheerful heart is like good medicine, but a broken spirit saps a person's strength...."* It is found in Proverbs 17, verse 22. When looked at with an inquisitive eye, the verse shows a contrast in experiences—a *cheerful heart* and a *broken spirit*. The latter is not necessarily an experience we choose—as caregivers. It is an experience which exists in the caregiver's reality. The spirit is broken during this journey of caregiving—no doubt. However, it does not need to be an irreparable brokenness. An extreme move towards the negative would be submerging into deep depression from which you will never recover. I believe I have matched these contrasting realities with an acronym that I want to recommend at this juncture:

The acronym is **H – E – A – L.**

The "H" represents – **Honor**. I considered it an honor to have the assignment to take care of my mother all the way to her final breath. We decided as a family that we would not move her into a facility to be cared for by strangers; they would hardly take care of her the way her family could. This is not to imply that it was an easy journey. Not at all. But the honor will always be felt for the rest of my life. Many times, the most complicated places to be, are in places of honor.

The "E" represents – **Envisioning**…envisioning life after the caregiving journey. It is a journey which does not last forever. Another favored scripture in the Bible says: *"Weeping may endure for a night, but joy comes in the morning"* (Psalm 30:5). This is a given. Although there may be sadness, loss, even grieving, that period *does* end! And there is indeed light at the end of the caregiving tunnel.

Envision or just imagine having joy again, after giving care to your loved one(s) and please know that the sad moments last only for a while. For the strongest of us caregivers—those *Rocks of Gibraltar*—we learn how to devise ways to have happy moments and even complete happy days here and there. We have constant emotional support—like family and friends who send a card if they're far away. We invite the friends and supporters of our loved ones—even throughout the Hospice seasons—to share a conversation, even over Facetime®, Zoom, and other technological means. We just need to be creative—believe me, filling your time with planning to communicate with others becomes just as fulfilling as the actual communication. So, include others in the journey and make as many happy moments as possible.

The "A" is for – **Acceptance**. Once we have taken on the task of caregiving, there is no reneging. There's no turning back. Taking on the responsibility is, in and of itself, fully accepting the responsibility. However, this *"acceptance"* refers mainly to the mental and cognitive acceptance of the responsibility of caregiving.

This responsibility is not for weaklings without backbones; it is certainly not for indecisive and undependable personalities. I believe there should be an award occasion devised and created just for honoring caregivers. We are indeed a special breed.

The "L" is for – **Life**. That is, living again after the caregiving journey. Having experienced this journey firsthand, it is my sheer pleasure to encourage you in the fact that there is indeed life after caregiving. For those who have been there as well (my partners in experience) I lock fingers of agreement and say, "Kudos! We made it!"

For some, it may have required therapy and counseling before, during and even after the journey, but we made it!

The process of healing is so critically necessary, that I would be remiss to not recommend at least several ways to begin healing in your caregiving journey.

Some options are:

(1) Find a few minutes of clean comedy that will make you laugh out loud!

Pulling up YouTube comedic performances. There are many clean-yet-hilarious comedians with their videos on YouTube.

(2) Calling or connecting with a friend or family member who is caring and funny to make you laugh.

(3) Watching a very funny movie. ELF is one of my favorites! Although it is obviously a Christmas movie, I have watched it at various times of the year, and laughed so hard each time, you would think it was my very first time watching it.

(4) Try writing a funny piece…a poem, a dialogue between two characters, or a short story—fictional or non-fictional.

(5) Read a book that has hilarious moments in it, that make you laugh out loud,

(6) Laughing will do wonders for you. Do it often!

(7) Vacation/Get-Away. As a resident of Florida, USA, for over 35 years at this point, I think Florida has more choices of get-away venues than any of the other states in America. The phrase "*Stay-cation*" was recently coined and fits perfectly into this recommendation. If, in your state or country there are options for getting-away inexpensively and for short periods of time, please utilize that as well.

Reflection Party

One year, or thereabouts, after the passing of your loved one, plan to have a **Reflection Party…** a virtual or in-person gathering of family and friends, to remember your loved one…

Recommendations:

-Go through your phone and make a list of all the people you want to include in the planning as well as those whom you will invite to the actual event.

You can have this at a location—like your home—where you can inexpensively make this happen. Another option is to set up a Virtual Gathering (using any of the current platforms). Also, you can plan a more expensive get-away gathering at a resort or similar venue to invite select attendees including family members and friends.

Write the Detailed Plan for Your **Reflections Party**

_____
_____
_____
_____
_____
_____
_____
_____
_____
_____
_____

CONCLUSION

During my journey of caring for my mother, I had friends and colleagues who were also going through similar experiences. While we were indeed caring for parents and loved ones around the same time, it was also a fact that we had similar, yet different experiences.

Remember that as much as we love our folks and would love for them to stay here with us forever, that is not realistic. What has helped me throughout—even the times when I still really, really miss both my parents—is to thank God for the fact that they lived for the number of years they did, and I had the honor of being a part of their lives—and vise-versa. My parents were both in their eighties when they passed away. They both lived very full lives, which is the reason we can have such rich memories of them. Those memories will transcend my generation, into the next—for their grandchildren to enjoy and pass down to even the next generations beyond that.

Those people with rich heritages should share it with the next several generations, I think. It becomes a part of your history, your story, your legacy. Remember that if we do not preserve and secure historical data, the next generations will be robbed of it.

And who was it that asked, *"If you don't know where you came from, how can you know who you are, and where you're going."* Maybe it was a declaration and not a question, but, either way it's a sobering and true statement.

Remember, our loved ones were **not** meant to be worshipped—but to be loved to the best of our ability. There is a difference. And I thank God every day that my experience with both my parents were positive ones. I am now able to live embracing a certain standard—in so many things—because of my parents. They were unselfish, giving, loving, and carried much integrity. They were absolutely great parents! Even in the times we disagreed they were great parents! They taught us great value structure and to live wonderful, respectable lives.

However, I believe that if upon their loss I had sunk into a deep and complete depression, and became hopeless and suicidal, then I would have needed to check my motives, and my underlying reasoning. It could have been from (1) my having held them at too high an esteem where it became more like a form of worship; or, (2) my not considering *their* needs in their latter years—and the fact that they may not have wanted to exist in a wheelchair totally dependent on others to care for them—as loving as that care may have been; or, (3) from guilt—the guilt of not having given them their flowers while they lived.

Of all the methodologies, the techniques, the therapeutic experiences, and all the strategies put in place to make the caregiver's experience a livable and endurable journey, the things that will make it all worth the while are the lessons learned. I think that all courageous caregivers should be given the opportunity to experience the general practice of men and women who have crossed over the victory line in their fight against drug addictions and alcoholism: We should be given the chance to go into a huge crowd, to stand up in that huge gathering and declare: *"Hello, my name is so-and-so, and I AM A CAREGIVER!"*

Why? Because caregiving is a difficult task! A difficult journey that takes courage beyond compare.

Across the board in this experience, there are valuable lessons learned… about your loved one(s), about yourself, and about the art of caregiving overall, that could not have been learned had you not taken the journey. There is nothing like personally experiencing a thing, then gaining the ability and power to help someone else by teaching them the ins and outs of it.

Most importantly, during the caregiving journey, make sure you take every step necessary to maintain your sanity by taking it one day at a time. Revisit the memories in this book—your *Caregiver's Journal—and* let it be a source of solace and strength for you. Let it be your reservoir of memories.

May God bless you immensely!

-Jascinth Brockington

Works Cited

---

(1) New King James Version (NKJV)
Scripture taken from the New King James Version®. Copyright © 1982 by Thomas Nelson. Used by permission. All rights reserved.

(2) www.BetterUp.com (March 3, 2022)

(3) New Living Translation (NLT) Holy Bible, New Living Translation, copyright © 1996, 2004, 2015 by Tyndale House Foundation, Carol Stream, IL 60188

Made in the USA
Columbia, SC
15 January 2024

3b26b401-2673-4620-92be-e5ee3921fcb5R01